JESUS IS A BALLER

JESUS IS A BALLER

Reflections on the
Fundamentals of Basketball

Elijah N. Gurash

LUMINARE PRESS
WWW.LUMINAREPRESS.COM

Jesus Is a Baller: Reflections on the Fundamentals of Basketball
Copyright © 2023 by Elijah N. Gurash

All rights reserved. This book or any portion thereof may not be reproduced or used in any manner whatsoever without the express written permission of the publisher, except for the use of brief quotations in a book review.

Printed in the United States of America

Luminare Press
442 Charnelton St.
Eugene, OR 97401
www.luminarepress.com

LCCN: 2023903454
ISBN: 979-8-88679-231-7

For Xander, Ollie, and Isla Grace.
And for my dad, thank you.

Contents

Introduction: The Weak Hand 1

PART ONE: SHOOTING

    Chapter 1: The Lay-Up 7

    Chapter 2: Midrange Jumper (Part 1) 13

    Chapter 3: Midrange Jumper (Part 2) 16

    Chapter 4: Beyond the Arc 26

PART TWO: BALL HANDLING

    Chapter 5: Driving to the Bucket 35

    Chapter 6: Relieving Pressure 42

    Chapter 7: Creating a Better Pass 48

PART THREE: PASSING

    Chapter 8: The Bounce Pass 55

    Chapter 9: The Chest Pass 59

PART FOUR: RECEIVING THE PASS

    Chapter 10: Triple Threat 65

Thank You 71

About the Author 75

Introduction

The Weak Hand

The summer of 1991 turned out to be the pivotal point of my basketball career. I had just completed 6th grade, and was living outside of Fresno, California. I spent most of my days playing basketball by myself, with friends, or with my dad. Since the weather was conducive to hitting the blacktop year-round, it was pure joy to own nothing but shorts to complete my wardrobe.

When my dad and I hit the playground we would work on a ton of shooting drills and always ended up playing a number of 1-on-1 games. Despite losing every single time, I ate it up. I loved the challenge and the competitive nature of our matchups. I went from getting skunked to making it close every once in a while. My confidence increased, and soon I began experimenting with odd finishes and off-balance shots. It was absolute fun and provided some amazing bonding experiences with my father.

One day we were at the park, which was within walking distance of our house, finishing up some shooting. My mom was hanging out at the swing sets, having pushed my sister there in the stroller. My dad and I started our daily game of 1-on-1. I don't remember a particular moment from that game, but I do recall the intensity. For the first time, I was within striking distance of a win. The game became crazy physical, and every single point was hotly contested. There was shoving, sweat, and a few scrapes from crashing to the asphalt. It was clear my dad was not backing down, and I became determined to give everything I had to get the win.

Game point must have been a bloodbath. Again, I don't recall the particulars, but I do know I hit the game-winner. I walked away victorious. However, there was no joy in the moment for anyone. My dad and I were at each other's throats. He walked away as mad as I have ever seen him. I walked away incensed at how intense he had become in the contest. Winning the game was more like surviving than anything else.

My dad started trudging home. I followed a good fifty yards behind him. My mom and sister were a good fifty yards behind me. Upon returning home, I noticed my mom's eyes were huge, having watched the entire encounter. She wisely left each of us alone. For the next three days my father and I lived in the same house without so much as looking at each other, let alone speaking. I'm not sure how my mother navigated that, but she did.

On the afternoon of the fourth day my dad asked if I wanted to go to the park and play basketball. I said yes. We didn't speak on our way there and we didn't speak as we went through our shooting routines. He rebounded and passed, just as I do with my sons now. At the end, he asked me if I was ready to play 1-on-1. I said yes. He approached me and explained there would be a new rule: I was only allowed to dribble and shoot with my left hand, my weak hand. That was the stimulus that turned me into a college basketball player.

PART ONE

SHOOTING

CHAPTER 1

THE LAY-UP

My earliest basketball memories place me in Wilmington, Ohio. My father was the youth pastor at the Methodist church. I absolutely loved Wilmington. I was about eight years old and our family had spent the previous three years or so in the middle of nowhere: Five Mile, Ohio. My father had been the head pastor of a small country church in Five Mile, and there was NOTHING to do! I was homeschooled, partly due to the one-hour bus ride to and from the elementary school. My days consisted of my mother and I working on reading, writing, and math, along with just trying to stave off the boredom. There were few kids, and even fewer play dates. I learned to ride my bike in the church graveyard, mow the grass on a riding John Deere, and play "ghost man" Wiffle ball with my folks.

After this, Wilmington was a breath of fresh air. I found myself surrounded by kids, and was able to play everywhere I went. The neighborhood was full of activity, the church was enormous, and we lived in an actual town. I loved the youth group. It was like a second family. I had survived the wandering of the desert, to be sat down in the promised land!

On top of everything, the church had a nice little indoor half-court, which was easily the coolest thing I had ever seen. The kids in the youth group would play often, and I spent time running around the court pretending to be involved in the action. One time, I even remember sneaking up behind my dad while he was dribbling and stealing the ball to thunderous applause. An interest in the game certainly started there, but it's not the setting of the most poignant and vivid experience of my early playing career.

My parents signed me up for youth basketball, which I'm sure consisted of one contest a week. I don't remember any practices, and I only really remember one game because of the conversation my dad and I had leading up to it. We discussed the lay-up. My father explained that while I was dribbling to the basket, I could pick the ball up and take two steps, jumping to shoot off the second step. I was in shock! That statement went against everything I had known about the game up to that point, which was basically that you had to dribble while moving. How could these two steps possibly be allowed?

Thinking back now, I realize I found myself in a quandary. In the heat of the game, I came up the court on a breakaway to the basket. At that moment the conversation with my dad raced through my head and the questions came even faster.

Can I take two steps? Is it true? Will the whistle blow for a travel call?

It was all too much to bear. In the end, I did not

take the two steps. I simply stopped dribbling and shot the ball. I missed the basket. I didn't trust my dad.

The lay-up is the first fundamental shot learned by all basketball players. It is the starting point of shooting. A child is taught how to hold the ball, how to place their feet and bend their knees, and how to extend their arm and follow through ("hand in the cookie jar"). That first opportunity to put it all into practice is standing to the side of the rim, aiming at that square, and giving it all you can to heave it into the basket. Once you make some progress, the two-step lay-up is introduced, allowing that little body to capitalize on some momentum. This is where my first failure took place—I didn't trust the instruction. And maybe a game isn't the best time to try something new, but we don't always get to control the setting and the circumstances of our lessons.

The game of basketball is the perfect metaphor for one's walk with God. The shot is the trajectory, the relationship, the culmination of experiences we have with God. It is the visual representation of the commitment of our lives to Him. And our relationship with God, no matter how old you are when accepting Jesus Christ as Lord and Savior, starts with the fundamentals. It starts with the lay-up. The lay-up is the beginning of your faith and trust in God.

Shooting a lay-up contains multiple stages of movement: two steps while securing the basketball, placing the hands in the proper spots, jumping off one foot, extending the shooting arm, and following through with the shooting hand. Mistakes in this process can lead to a miss and the need to learn, adjust, and try again. Many stages of our relationship with Jesus can have similar challenges. There are plenty of moving parts in our lives: family, school/work, friendships, and various responsibilities, to name a few. Somehow in that early walk we must learn to decipher God's will for our lives amid the world around us. We make mistakes, give in to old habits, or fail repeatedly in one or more aspects of our new lives. The result is being off target in our relationship with God. It takes time and practice. Thankfully, God is patient and gracious and always there to pick us up when we stumble.

First Peter 2:2 states "as newborn babes, desire the pure milk of the word, that you may grow thereby." God provides the instruction manual in His Word, the Bible. Not only that, but He provides Himself as a loving Father and Teacher to guide us. He is so encouraging, always there to forgive and provide support. On our end, though, we must desire the instruction and trust His Word even when we do not always understand what we read in the Bible. Proverbs 3:5 declares that we are to "Trust in the Lord with all your heart, and lean not on your own understanding." It can be difficult to follow that directive during our spiritual infancy, especially when we are used to relying on ourselves. That is where I flunked for the first of many times.

I could not understand the concept of the lay-up and therefore could not trust what my dad was instructing me to do. The result in the moment was a missed shot. However, the opportunity to learn from the mistake was invaluable. My dad didn't jump down my throat or discipline me for not listening to him. In fact, I don't remember the subject even coming up after the game. As time passed, I became aware of my need to listen and trust my father, and he was always gracious enough to work with me. Our Father in heaven is that and so much more. I eventually mastered the lay-up, and now, thirty-five years later, I find myself in the position of the father instructing his children.

One of the true joys of my life is taking my two boys out to the park and working with them on their basketball skills. My youngest son, Ollie, is working on mastering the lay-up. He is learning to trust the two steps and is gaining a handle on all the moving parts. It has pushed me to explain the process and break down the components of the lay-up into separate, manageable chunks. We started at the ground level, and it is so much fun to watch his confidence grow and see the joy on his face as the ball swishes through the basket. During these moments, I can't help but think of my own dad and the time we spent together. He must have treasured it, so how much more must our Father in heaven treasure the moments when we trust and grow in our relationship with Him?

Proverbs 22:6 instructs us to "train up a child in the way he should go, and when he is old he will not depart from it." I look at my life and where I am with my walk with God, as well as where I am at the park shooting hoops with my boys. I know a lay-up seems simple, but it is the starting point for things which are much grander. It is fundamental, the rock upon which to build. My dad started me on my journey in faith and in hoops. God used him to help give me the solid foundation I needed. My relationship with my Savior, Jesus Christ, is the most important thing in my life, but it wouldn't be possible without the basics. Thanks to my love of basketball, I see that the purity of a beautiful shot is a wonderful metaphor for our walk with Christ. And that walk must start somewhere: the lay-up.

CHAPTER 2

MIDRANGE JUMPER (PART 1)

Two thoughts immediately come to mind when I think about the midrange jump shot. The first is my oldest son, Xander, and our continuous work on his shot from about twelve to sixteen feet out. Xander has put in considerable time on his jumper. We have already spent years hammering away at the mechanics and correcting little inconsistencies in his shooting form. Every time we step out to shoot, we must adjust components of his shot that have slipped. There are so many parts to the jump shot, and they involve the entire body. When one tiny area is not doing its part, the ball refuses to go in. On the other hand, when everything is working in rhythm and the ball rips through the net, it is an absolute thing of beauty.

If the lay-up represents the beginning of our walk with Christ, then the midrange jumper is the adolescent part of the journey. We know enough about God to understand the basics of our faith, to recall and recite biblical stories and how they relate to our circumstances, and we have come to truly believe He loves us. But, at the same time, we are in a constant fight. We are faced with attacks from the enemy, from others, and from ourselves. Some of the mercies that protected us in our spiritual infancy have been exchanged for genuine contact with the real world.

As a father, I relish the time I spend rebounding for my son and watching him shoot. I love giving him notes and watching him apply the information and feel the success. His confidence grows in front of my eyes. However, I must balance that interaction and not become overbearing or too protective, isolating him from the game itself. He's on a great team, with a great coach, and I have purposefully taken a step back to give him freedom to experience success and failure without standing over him the entire time. It's tough! I hate to see him struggle in a game or miss shots I know he can make. It has been agonizing to observe from the stands as he learns painful lessons. But it is so amazing to see him correct his own mistakes (maybe the mechanics of his shot) and fight through the adversity in real live action and embrace accomplishment on the other side. It really is Proverbs 22:6 in action, watching the training take hold in his life, knowing that the difficulties will only ensure that he will not depart from it.

This process has made me understand my Father in heaven even more. If I can see this in a thirteen-year-old playing basketball, how much more does God see in each of us? He knows the gifts He's given us and the struggles we face. He knows the outcome and how each step of adversity is there to make each of us stronger, resilient to use those gifts for His kingdom. It certainly isn't easy, and there are many moments of tears, but God is always there walking with us. He uses EVERYTHING for good! So, every moment is an opportunity for Him to console us, to correct us, to strengthen us, to enlighten us, or to discipline us. It is exhausting and frustrating, but it is also the point in life when our faith grabs hold, and we start to become who we are meant to be. Hebrews 5:12–14 describes this conflict in different terms:

> For though by this time you ought to be teachers, you need someone to teach you again the first principles of the oracles of God; and you have come to need milk and not solid food. For everyone who partakes only of milk is unskilled in the word of righteousness, for he is a babe. But solid food belongs to those who are of full age, that is, those who by reason of use have their senses exercised to discern both good and evil.

CHAPTER 3

MIDRANGE JUMPER (PART 2)

My second thought regarding the midrange jump shot entails Jesus personally rebounding for me as I worked on my jumper. I know it sounds crazy, but let me share the entire story before you pass judgment. It was the 2013–14 academic year, and I was well past my playing days. I was deep into coaching, with a wife and two young sons at home, and in almost every facet of my life, I was at rock bottom.

We were living in my hometown of Fairmont, West Virginia. My wife Katy stayed at home with our boys, residing in a house owned by my parents. They were gracious enough to let us live there rent free. Every day I traveled an hour to and from my teaching and coaching job several school districts away. We were down to one vehicle, eking out an existence. On top of mental and physical exhaustion, financial stress and parenting responsibilities, my wife and I were depleted in our attempts to even coexist in a healthy manner.

"Going around the mountain" was my metaphor to explain what our marriage was like. We had the same arguments every few weeks or months. The topic might be different each time, but the argument was always the same. It could be set off by just about anything, and no matter what changes we vowed to make, we would eventually go around the mountain again. We read books, listened to sermons, went deep into discussions and prayer, and tried our best to make things better. It all seemed to lead nowhere.

Looking back now, I can see God was at that point where He had allowed the struggle, watching as I searched deeply for Him and grounded myself in my Christian foundation. It was undoubtedly one of the toughest stretches of my life. While these internal and external battles were occurring, my parents were hosting a minister for a few days. He was there to pray with anyone in the family who wanted to sit down with him, happy to spend time connecting with God and declaring freedom from the generational bondage that was affecting our lives. Katy and I both were eager for the opportunity.

Everyone had a private session with the minister, and mine had quite the surprise ending. The session was good, and I did feel some weight taken off my shoulders, but our closing prayer time was astonishing. As he was praying for me, he felt God interrupt him. He said, "God is telling me that you are Elijah. You are not Eli, but Elijah. Yes."

He explained that God, on occasion, changes names, and that he had encountered this a couple of times while praying for individuals. I was in shock. I believed what he said to be true, but I still had a difficult time wrapping my head around it.

When I shared this with my wife and parents, my father pointed out that it was not unbiblical. There were many people in Scripture who went through a name change at God's direction. That was comforting. In addition, my parents shared that they always considered my name, Eli, to be short for Elijah. Before my birth, they apparently discussed giving me the name Elijah but calling me Eli. However, before they fully solidified their course of action, my mother was rushed to the hospital. It was a month before my due date, and the doctors had minutes to save both of our lives. My mother was bleeding internally. I was born via emergency C-section, and my mother survived. My father, in agony throughout the ordeal, was left to handle the paperwork after we both came out in good health. Due to his frazzled emotional state, he put "Eli" down on the birth certificate. At this point, I could at least begin to connect some dots with a name change to "Elijah." Nevertheless, I was unable to commit to the change. Something was holding me back.

Some time passed, and as great as it was to spend those moments in prayer with that pastor, we eventually began rounding the mountain again. I was shattered, combing through Christian texts, asking God for anything that would help our family. I became convinced that one author, Charles Kraft, had what we were looking for. His book, *Deep Healing*, spoke to everything we were going through. We tried to apply his concepts, but to no avail. I desperately began searching through the California White Pages, calling every Charles Kraft in the book, hoping to connect with this man. I never found him. But, through my online searching, I found a woman who had been trained by Charles Kraft. She specialized in deep healing. I called and emailed immediately.

A few days later, I received a call from the husband-and-wife team of Mack and Catherine Harris. I broke down crying in my car, explaining the situation my wife and I were in. They listened intently, compassionately, and said, "We can work with that."

If I was crying before, I was sobbing at this point. I was so desperate for help. I was sick of fighting on my own and gaining no ground. I felt helpless and alone. And God showed up!

We put together a logistical plan, and during Thanksgiving week, my wife flew out to California to meet with Mack and Catherine and go through deep healing counseling. I stayed home with the boys, taking Xander to basketball practices while my folks watched Ollie. It was a tough week on my end. Ollie got sick, and the three of us struggled through each day. I only spoke to Katy a couple times that entire week. She was involved in intensive all-day sessions, and the three-hour time difference wreaked havoc on our schedules. She flew back on Thanksgiving Day, in time for our family dinner.

What she went through, what she was healed from, is her story to tell. What I can bear witness to on my end is she came back a different person. She did not share much, but shared enough to give me an idea of what her sessions were like. She reached out to me and said, "Thank you." That stood out the most. Unsurprisingly, I was quite reluctant at first. I kept my distance, waiting to see when we would round the mountain again. But weeks passed, then months, and she was still different. Katy was herself, but she was the best version of herself. The edge I had been grappling with for years was no longer there. It was as unsettling as it was refreshing. By the time basketball season ended, I was ready to go to California.

My first session started with me bringing up the idea of a name change. I explained what had taken place seven months prior and how I had been struggling with committing to changing my name to Elijah. It was foremost on my mind, so we dug in. Catherine shared a personal story which dealt with name changes. I listened and understood, but one thing stumped me as we were talking. I shared that nothing bothered me about my name, Eli, and how that fact was holding me back.

She looked intently at me and asked, "Is there anything from your life—anything at all, no matter how minor it may seem—that has ever bothered you about your name?"

It was like a lightning bolt struck me. My eyes widened and I said "Yes."

At that moment, I recalled being young and always hating the biblical story of Eli and his two wicked sons. It bothered me that Eli was not a flattering figure from

Scripture, and that his legacy was so rotten. As I spoke those words, it hit me that I was Eli, father to two sons. I nodded in acknowledgment of this twist of fate and decided to commit to my new name.

That evening, back in my hotel room, I went through my phone and sent every person in my contact list a message explaining that I would now be going by the name Elijah. After sending the last text out, an earthquake hit. I sat in bed, rocking back and forth, astonished by the timing of it all. The next day, I discovered it was a 4.5 quake, with the epicenter having been in the area. I took some time to read that morning from a biography on Samuel written by F. B. Meyer. In the one page I managed to get through, Meyer referenced the time Samuel stood praying on behalf of the Israelites as they faced the Philistines. This was before David or Saul even entered the picture. The Lord answered and brought His presence into the battle, causing the Philistines to stumble as though in an earthquake. The Israelites pounced and defeated their enemy. Reading that story, I thought, was not a coincidence. I was anxious to share all of this with Catherine, and as I was doing so a couple hours later, an aftershock rumbled through the building—that made three earthquake-related events or stories, all perfectly timed with my decision. I don't think God allowed the earthquake just for my benefit, but He certainly used the timing of it all to speak to me directly. I have been Elijah ever since.

My next counseling session brought me face to face with what I knew to be the greatest source of my pain from my younger years. The United States Military Academy at West Point is about as prestigious as it gets, and I had accepted an offer to attend and play basketball for the Black Knights. At eighteen, it was a dream come true. I worked hard to have the opportunity to play Division I college basketball and attend a highly respected academic institution which would set me up for success as an adult. What I did not know, and could not have known ahead of time, was how crushing the environment would prove to be for me.

That year was the most arduous of my life. Surviving Beast Barracks, the nine months of hazing, countless push-ups and sit-ups, and pinging around the grounds like an idiot while being overloaded academically was intense, to say the least. On top of all the crazy academy responsibilities, adding basketball to the mix and existing on five hours of sleep each night soon took its toll. There are several stories I could tell about that year, but the main point is I was miserable. My soul was crushed, my confidence was shattered, and I spent most days repeatedly praying "God help me."

The basketball court has always been home, and it was the one refuge for me during that year, as I was blessed to play a ton as a freshman. I shot well that year: 41 percent from beyond the arc. But that season became a strain, just like the rest of academy life. The long hours and loss of my personal identity wore on me. The culture was confusing, and the team chemistry was lacking. The leadership was poor and morale was miserable. I suffered considerable emotional and mental anguish that year, and for a solid fifteen years, I carried the wounds of that experience with me everywhere.

I went into detail with Catherine, sharing story after story of my time at West Point. It was unbelievable how much had been bottled up inside me. It just kept pouring out. After hours of releasing it all, Catherine asked, "Are you ready to give it over to Jesus?"

I absolutely was!

I closed my eyes and found myself sitting on the couch in my coach's office at Army. This moment was somewhere between a memory, a vision, and a dream. It is hard to explain. But as I pictured myself sitting there, I saw Jesus sitting beside me. He held a sword across His lap, and it was comforting to have Him there. As I explained what I was seeing, Catherine asked if I was ready to start giving my hurts to Jesus. I began to ask forgiveness and to renounce individual moments and emotions from that year. Each of these components took the form of a piece of paper, and as I handed each paper to Jesus, it fell between His legs, across the sword on His lap, splitting in two before falling to the ground. For example, I asked forgiveness for the guilt I felt about leaving West Point after that year. I renounced that guilt, and it took the form of a paper that fell at Jesus' feet. I left shame, anger, and a mountain of other emotions at His feet. The pile became quite large. In one instance, I even handed Him a glass, which shattered as it fell across the sword.

It represented being told that year that I was a "glass-half-empty person." I never realized how much that remark cut me. To make matters worse, I believed that lie about myself for a decade and a half.

When that part of the spiritual exercise ended, Jesus stood up and lowered the point of His sword onto the pile. It burst into flame and disintegrated. All of it was gone. He motioned for me to follow Him, and we left the office and entered the gym. I revealed what was taking place to Catherine, and she explained that He was going to replace what He had just destroyed. Jesus led me to a side hoop off the main court. It was the hoop I most often shot at during practice drills. I felt comfortable there. Jesus stood under the basket and passed a ball to me. I began to put up shots from the wing. Jesus kept rebounding and kicking the ball back out. I would cut, catch, and release over and over. It was such an amazing experience; Jesus was rebounding for me!

After a time, He walked up and faced me. I was sweaty and at peace. He drew the sword from his belt and presented it to me. I took it by the handle, honored to have it. I shared with Catherine what was taking place, confused by what it meant. She chuckled, clarifying that this sword was my personal "sword of the Spirit." What was meant to destroy me in that year of my life, the fire that I went through, Jesus used to forge that very sword. What the enemy meant for destruction Jesus used for creation. All the hurts and wounds I carried for so long, Jesus extinguished with that very sword, and He was giving it to me. My battlefield was the basketball court and He was encouraging and equipping me for the plans He had—and still has—for me. In an instant, I was no longer Eli ("the highest"), walking through life wounded, fighting battles on my own for my own glory. I had become Elijah ("my God is Yahweh"), whole and fighting with the sword of the Spirit for God's glory.

First Peter 1:6–7 states, "In this you greatly rejoice, though now for a little while, if need be, you have been grieved by various trials, that the genuineness of your faith, being much more precious than gold that perishes, though it is tested by fire, may be found to praise, honor, and glory at the revelation of Jesus Christ."

My year at West Point put me on an extremely long and difficult road filled with years of heartache and adversity. There were plenty of highlights during those fifteen years, but I experienced it all in a wounded state. This exemplifies the adolescent years of walking with God. We all have a story, good times and bad. We face obstacles, all used by God to solidify our faith. We walk through the fire to come out stronger on the other end, ready and willing to answer the call God has on our lives. It isn't easy, but it's worth it. It is the midrange jumper. It takes years to perfect, and there are times of agony in the process. But in the end, the shot is on target.

CHAPTER 4

BEYOND THE ARC

Larry Bird, Reggie Miller, Steve Kerr, Ray Allen, and Steph Curry all come to mind when you start to discuss the best shooters to ever play basketball. Each of these players have hit clutch shots in clutch moments to propel their teams to victory. They are or were consistent over many seasons, and very reliable from beyond the arc. That being said, none of them have a career three-point shooting percentage above 50 percent. The best of the best have more misses on their resumés than makes, and that stat is significant for a couple reasons. One, it shows how difficult it is to make shots from beyond the arc. And two, it speaks to the confidence and work ethic of these all-time greats, who have experienced (statistically speaking) more failure than success while claiming their places in the record books.

I enjoyed growing up with and watching these NBA sharpshooters, but never had the opportunity to grind out a season with any of them. However, during the 2019–20 season at Whitworth University I had the privilege of sitting on the bench and watching the most dominant display of shooting I have ever witnessed.

As an assistant coach, it was my honor to enjoy a front-row seat to the Ben College Show:

> College averaged 22.9 points per game this season, which ranked 23rd in Division III. He also led the Northwest Conference, and ranked second in the nation, in free throw percentage (91.6). On Feb. 29th he became the third player in Whitworth history to surpass 1,800 career points and he finished with 1,863, which is now second on the Pirates' all-time scoring list. Only Whitworth Heritage Gallery Hall-of-Famer Bryan Depew, who scored 2,013 points from 2001–04, is ahead of him on the list. College broke the Pirates' single season record for three-pointers made (99) in 2019–20 and Whitworth's career record for free throw percentage (88.4%). He set Whitworth's single-game record for three-pointers made (11) twice in his career, including a game this year at PLU. College established a career-high of 44 points in that win at PLU on February 1st and became the first Whitworth player to score 40+ points twice in a season since Rod McDonald in 1966.[1]
>
> Excerpt from Whitworthpirates.com

Ben can absolutely shoot the rock! And that game against Pacific Lutheran University was something

---

[1] Excerpt from Whitworthpirates.com.

to behold. Our entire offense turned into "Ben, what play do you want to run?" He was unstoppable, hitting highly contested shots from well beyond the NBA's three-point line. It was a thing of beauty. More importantly, it was not coincidence or luck. It was the result of a lot of hard work.

You could ask any player in our program to name the hardest worker, and they would all point to Ben College. Ben routinely put together a summer program that had him logging more than 20,000 made buckets. And during the academic year, including in season, he would routinely make 1,000 shots a week on his own time. He put in the work, seeing the ball rim out more than it went in, grinding on his craft and holding himself accountable to the highest standard. This gave him the confidence, when the lights were on, to excel. He put the time in and reaped the rewards of his labor.

That brings us back to the metaphor of shooting and how it relates to our relationship with God. Establishing one's self as a great three-point shooter takes a ton of hours in the gym. It starts by first working close to the rim, progressing out to midrange, and eventually crafting accuracy from extreme distance. There is no shortcut. It takes time and effort. Similarly, there is no shortcut in a relationship with God. It takes time and effort as well.

Years of walking with God, experiencing the highs and lows of life, brings us into a deeper faith with the Almighty. He crafts us and shapes us through it all. And as our roots grow deep into our foundation in Christ, our confidence and understanding in life grows as well. We learn lessons and continue to cultivate our identity in Him. Through this process our faith becomes strong, and faith is what allows the trajectory of our lives to be straight and true, honing in on that spiritual basket. For Hebrews 11:6 states, "But without faith it is impossible to please Him, for he who comes to God must believe that He is, and that He is a rewarder of those who diligently seek Him."

Hebrews 11 goes on to recount the faith of major biblical figures and events, starting almost every example with the same phrase:

"By faith Abel…" (verse 4)

"By faith Enoch…" (verse 5)

"By faith Noah…" (verse 7)

"By faith Abraham…" (verse 8)

"By faith Sarah…" (verse 9)

"By faith Isaac…" (verse 20)

"By faith Jacob…" (verse 21)

"By faith Joseph…" (verse 22)

"By faith Moses…" (verse 23)

"By faith the walls of Jericho fell down…" (verse 30)

"By faith the harlot Rahab…" (verse 31)

> "And what more shall I say? For time would fail me to tell of Gideon and Barak and Samson and Jephthah, and also of David and Samuel and the prophets." (verse 32)

Faith is not only the component that is shared in each of these examples, it is the lifeblood. It is the heart and soul of an eternal relationship with God. Because of faith, God worked powerfully in each of these lives and they each sit in heaven today.

When a basketball player pulls up to take a three-point shot in a game, he or she is exercising faith to its maximum. Hebrews 11:1 tell us, "Faith is the substance of things hoped for, the evidence of things not seen." That shooter is hoping the ball will go in. That hope is built on hours of intimate time in the gym. There is evidence from past efforts that the ball can go in. The hours of practice have built trust that, if performed correctly, the shooting motion will result in a make. But there is no evidence in the heat of the contest, in the moment, that the ball will go in. The evidence is a thing not yet seen. The shot is taken in faith, confidently, because of the relationship built between the player, the ball, and the hoop.

However, we know that shot at best has less than a 50 percent chance of going in. The failure rate is pretty high. This is where I find the beauty in the metaphor. The people listed in Hebrews 11 exercised tremendous faith. Most of them delved deep into a faith that is hard to comprehend. And yet, each of these individuals experienced moments of utter failure. They were men and women that made huge mistakes. They suffered through lowly moments that included lying and cheating, committing adultery and murder, succumbing to anger issues and sexual desires, and giving in to flashes of extreme pride and selfishness. They were not perfect people exercising perfect faith. They were flawed people, just like us, humbling themselves before God because they knew how flawed they were.

These are giants of the faith who failed many times in their walk on this earth. They are relatable, and God still used them in profound ways despite their shortcomings. We often mess up and miss in our walk with God. Despite the hours spent with Him and the relationship that has been built, we still miss in our trajectory. Much like the shot from beyond the arc, our best day shooting doesn't even come close to perfect. Thankfully, God is perfect. He meets us on our good days and bad. Our job is to put in the time, to build our faith, to keep firing shots at the rim. We'll keep getting better, but we'll never be perfect. In fact, we'll fail more times than we succeed. Nevertheless, our confidence will grow in Christ. Our muscles, physically and spiritually, will grow stronger. Our faith will deepen exponentially.

PART TWO

BALL HANDLING

CHAPTER 5

DRIVING TO THE BUCKET

My father recently sent my two boys a present in the mail. He had found "Pistol" Pete Maravich's old basketball instructional videos in DVD format. The boys first asked who Pete Maravich was. After crossing that hurdle, I explained that these were the same videos their grandfather had gotten me when I was a kid. Of course, we had them on VHS. It was so cool that my dad had found the updated format version and sent them to his grandsons. We popped the first DVD in: "Dribbling."

We watched the first portion of the instruction, wrote down the sequence of the stationary dribbling drills, and prepared to go out to the driveway. The boys remarked that we had been doing several of the drills already. I concurred. It was funny; I hadn't thought about those videos for years, but somehow I was instructing my sons in a similar sequence. They continue working on their stationary ball handling, going through Pistol Pete's instruction.

The next phase in this basketball metaphor concerns dribbling and how we handle the ball on the court. No child starts out as a ball-handling wizard.

Just as in developing a shot, dribbling takes years of practice. There are no shortcuts. The arms, hands, and fingertips must develop a relationship with the ball and how it bounces on the court surface. In addition, it's imperative that this is done without looking at the basketball. A player must be able to dribble in a game, trusting the bounce of the ball while surveying the court and all the moving pieces on it.

In life, we must navigate the world around us: work, school, family, friends, hobbies, debts, and unforeseen obstacles. Our heads can't be pointed down, buried with blinders on. We must maneuver and trust. This trust comes from building a relationship. In the game, it is between the player and the ball; in life, in one's spiritual walk, it is between the person and God. This is done through daily reading of Scripture and through prayer.

As I watch my sons go through dribbling drills, I can't help but think about the discipline of daily Scripture reading and prayer. The only way to get better at handling a basketball is to practice dribbling a basketball. In the same vein, the way to dive deeper into a relationship with God is to spend time reading the Bible. It is imperative to know where God stands on all of the angles in life, and His Scripture provides that information. There is, however, one other giant similarity I have found between the dribbling drills and daily practice of reading Scripture: it is easy to skip.

There are certainly days when my boys complain about working on their dribbling. I often hear comments like, "It's so boring," "Let's not do it today," and "I just don't feel like it." And, if I'm honest with myself, I've said those same things about reading my Bible. It's not always easy, and there are always things that can disrupt intentions. Before you know it, a week has gone by without cracking open His Word. This is why I use the word "discipline" when connecting these two pursuits. It takes true discipline to improve one's ball handling. It takes true discipline to spend time each day reading Scripture and praying. The results from these commitments are well worth it.

The number one goal (concerning the use of the dribble) of any basketball player is to drive to the bucket. If a player is out of range for his or her jump shot, or if there is an open lane to attack, the dribble is vital in this pursuit. This is where we find out how much time has been spent on those drills. Either the drive to the hoop is under control, maintaining a solid dribble, or it is sporadic, lacking confidence, which likely results in losing possession of the basketball. Confidence is the key in this situation. Players who have spent time grinding away at this skill will have the confidence to attack the opening, knowing the ball will bounce as intended. Those who have not put in the work will lose the ball on the attack or won't even attempt it. All of those hours, dutifully spent or wasted, reveal themselves in an instant.

The same is true in our daily walk. The drive to the basket represents taking advantage of the opportunities that open up in our lives. God continuously opens and closes doors. Without reading His Word and spending time in prayer, it is easy to bobble an opportunity God has ordained or to allow it to pass by completely. Referencing Proverbs 3:5–6 again, "Trust in the Lord with all your heart, and lean not on your own understanding; in all your ways acknowledge Him, and He shall direct your paths." It takes time to learn how to lean less on our own understanding and lean more on Him. This is where daily discipline comes in.

As the years pass by, I become more and more aware of the importance of my daily habit of reading and prayer. When I stay plugged in, I feel God directing my path constantly. When I slip up and start to skip, I feel myself wandering on my own path. In simple terms, one path is peaceful, and one is not. And even when I am consciously walking with God daily, there are times when my own understanding gets in the way.

A few years ago I had a particular job opportunity placed at my doorstep on numerous occasions. The job would have supplemented my career in coaching, and by all accounts looked like a nice fit. But herein lies the catch: Is it what God wants for me? As I began asking God for wisdom in the decision, my daily reading habit came to the forefront. The very night that I wrestled greatly with the job opportunity I cracked open my Bible to read my daily passage. It happened to be 1 Kings, chapter 13. I was completely unfamiliar with the story. It involves a prophet and an old man who seemingly lies, resulting in a punishment that comes across as extremely severe. It is a story I'm sure I have read before, but just breezed by. This time, however, it struck like lightning. It made perfect sense with respect to the choice I was facing. And, for me, it was painfully obvious what choice I needed to make: pass on the job.

It was so intense to realize how intimately God connects. I had been reading my Bible for months without ever having a moment like this. And to think about how God directed my nightly reading quota so that I would read that story on that particular evening is mind-blowing. In addition, everything about the job seemed like a perfect fit. From my own understanding and from the world's perspective it looked like a no-brainer. For whatever reason, though, God told me no. Even crazier, the story doesn't end there.

As stated above, the job didn't just disappear. After declining the offer, some time passed and I was eventually offered it again. And again, I struggled with the decision. Everything about it pointed to a nice opening. I began praying once more, and that night I opened up my Bible to 2 Kings, chapter 23. King Josiah comes across the bones of the prophet and the old man, deciding not to disturb their resting place. God's providence is nothing short of spectacular. The odds of landing on that story, the only other passage about these two characters, on that night must be astronomical. I turned the job down once more. To this day I do not know why I wasn't supposed to take that opportunity. I only know that God made it clear to me not to. As I see it, my job is just to obey. Isaiah 55:8–9 sums it up:

> "For my thoughts are not your thoughts,
> Nor are your ways My ways," says the Lord.
> "For as the heavens are higher than the earth,
> So are My ways higher than your ways,
> And My thoughts than your thoughts."

God opens doors and closes doors. It's important to know which ones to walk through and which ones to walk away from. He has opened countless doors during my lifetime, and closed quite a few too. Reading Scripture and spending time in prayer allows one to discern the difference. The apostle Paul knew the importance of this on a few different levels. In Colossians 4:2–3 he pleads, "Continue earnestly in prayer, being vigilant in it with thanksgiving, meanwhile praying also for us, that God would open to us a door for the word, to speak the mystery of Christ…" In his evangelism, Paul counted on prayer to open the right doors. And in Corinthians 16:8–9 he explains, "But I will tarry in Ephesus until Pentecost. For a great and effective door has opened to me, and there are many adversaries."

Paul was praying and asking others to pray for him as he walked the path God intended for him. Regardless of the cost, Paul walked through the open doors with confidence. To drive the point home even further,

Paul even discovered that the door is sometimes literal. In Acts 16, Paul and Silas are in prison, bound in chains, when God generates an earthquake that sets them free and opens all the doors of the prison. The result of this miracle brings the warden of the prison and his entire family into the kingdom of God and allows Paul and Silas to walk free. I know Paul knew the power of walking through God's open doors.

CHAPTER 6

RELIEVING PRESSURE

Earlier I referenced the struggles Katy and I faced while living in West Virginia. Those struggles were immense and the healing that came out of the counseling that followed was life-changing. The point, however, that I want to expound on is that there were struggles on almost every front. Adversity met me on my doorstep daily. But through the adversity God drew me closer to Him.

There are a number of passages from 2 Corinthians underlined in my Bible. Every single one of those verses was highlighted during this time in my life. I could easily just insert the entire letter to drive home my point, but I will instead cite a few verses (starting with chapter 4, verses 16 through 18):

> Therefore we do not lose heart. Even though our outward man is perishing, yet the inward man is being renewed day by day. For our light affliction, which is but for a moment, is working for us a far more exceeding and eternal weight of glory, while we do not look at the things which are seen, but at the things which

> are not seen. For the things which are seen are temporary, but the things which are not seen are eternal.

I consider the strains of that period in my life "light afflictions." I did not suffer the loss of a loved one. I did not find myself jobless or homeless. I did not endure a debilitating disease. Many in life have been dealt these kinds of massive blows, and I believe these words in 2 Corinthians can bring comfort to such people. My afflictions seem trivial in comparison, but they were real for me, and God turned my difficulties into an opportunity to seek Him in an earnest way.

One particular struggle stands out as a prime example of how God meets us as we sincerely commit to the daily discipline of reading and prayer. My teaching/coaching job was several school districts away from where we lived in Fairmont. It was the only opening that God provided during that time, and it was fifty-five miles, door to door. Without going into all the particulars, our situation was such that we needed to live in Fairmont and I needed to drive those 110 miles each day.

Every workday started very early, but in the fall and spring I was able to get home in time for dinner and help coach my kids' soccer teams. It made for long days, for sure. The winter was a different story. The workday began the same. However, depending on practice times or game times for the basketball program, I would get home anywhere between 7pm and 11pm. There were a number of stretches where I only went home to sleep, not seeing my wife or kids for days on end.

Time away from family is common in the coaching profession. My wife and I understood that and made the most of it. What irritated me more than anything, however, were the two taxing, tiring hours in the car each day. Not to mention the times of driving home in a blizzard or sitting parked on the interstate for multiple hours because of a wreck. The monotony of the long drive and the frustration of losing time with my family drove me crazy.

I dove deep into my Bible, finding many words that gave me strength: "My brethren, count it all joy when you fall into various trials, knowing that the testing of your faith produces patience" (James 1:2–3). My patience certainly grew during those years and that drive had a lot to do with it. But I didn't get over the hump and find my peace in the circumstance until I studied the prophet Jeremiah. God used Jeremiah to speak to His people during times of hardship. Jeremiah was given words to spark the Israelites to return to their commitment to God. He had a tough job as most people did not want to hear the truth.

I have found that in my study of Scripture I often need to supplement my daily reading with a book on a particular subject. My favorite series of books, a number of which are character studies, are by F. B. Meyer. I read his book on Jeremiah as I read through the book of Jeremiah. The beginning of Jeremiah 13, verses 1 through 11, tells the story of Jeremiah and a linen sash. God directed Jeremiah to take a clean linen sash to the Euphrates River and bury it in a hole in the rocks. After completing the task and returning home, God directed Jeremiah to return to the Euphrates River, dig up the sash he had buried, and bring it home. The sash itself represented the demise of God's chosen people.

F. B. Meyer addressed one crucial aspect of this story that left me crushed. The distance from Jeremiah's location to the Euphrates River is around 250 miles. It wasn't just down the road! And, even more sobering, Jeremiah made the journey twice. Meyer explains this point in beautiful terms:

> The lesson of this double journey, which must have meant about a thousand miles on foot, teaches us that no exertion on our part should be considered excessive if we can execute the commissions of our King. Long before, when a comparative child, Jeremiah had been summoned to perform God's errands for Him, and it was not for him to complain if any special errand took him far afield, or involved journeying under scorching suns and sleeping in the night-dews. When Jesus bids us go into all the world, he means it, and we may not plead before him the distance and the hardships of the way. It is enough if He has said, "Go to Euphrates." When once we are sure of this

> we must imitate the prophet, who says, with charming simplicity, "So I went to Euphrates."[2]

I was humbled. I thought to myself, "If Jeremiah can walk a thousand miles without grumbling and complaining, surely I can manage this drive." It was a true "light bulb" moment. I prayed and asked forgiveness for all my moaning and frustration, and from that point on I quit whining and just made the most of it. A weight was lifted from my shoulders. The drive didn't magically get shorter; I just had a total new frame of reference for dealing with it. My time spent reading and studying brought a giant sense of relief. The pressure dissipated.

The connection of this point to the game of basketball is simple. As a ball handler, there are times when one must use the dribble to relieve pressure. The most common scenario would be the use of the retreat dribble as two defenders attempt a trap. The ball handler sees and senses multiple defenders approaching. At that moment, he/she must have confidence in the dribble to move backward while surveying the court. It is quite the opposite of attacking the basket. The goal of this tactic is to spread the defenders out even farther from one another, relieving pressure on offense while exposing openings or cracks within the defense. It can be unsettling to move in reverse with the basketball, putting stress on one's skill level in the face of adversity. That is why implementing a daily regimen of dribbling

---

[2] F. B. Meyer, *Jeremiah: Priest and Prophet*, Pg. 123

drills is so important: it allows a player to be successful in the face of intense pressure.

In the same way, spending time with God prepares us for adversity. It drives a person deeper into relationship with God, exposing the cracks in the enemy's defense. Second Corinthians 4:8–9 affirms, "We are hard-pressed on every side, yet not crushed; we are perplexed, but not in despair; persecuted, but not forsaken; struck down, but not destroyed." I felt hard-pressed and perplexed for sure in my commute. God drew me to Him and spoke through His Word, relieving pressure in an instant. The same feelings take place on the basketball court, and time spent committed to the craft helps alleviate that pressure.

CHAPTER 7

CREATING A BETTER PASS

If the first goal of ball handling is to drive to the basket, and the second goal is to relieve pressure, then the third is to create a better pass. There are many ways to describe this tenet: pick-and-roll, feeding the post, drive-and-kick, dribble handoffs, skips-and-drops, to name a few. Whatever the scenario, the point of the dribble remains the same: in each case, the ball handler uses the dribble to evade or engage the defense and create a passing angle to connect with a teammate. Every offense in the world has a scheme predicated on this principle. It's what makes the game great. Five individuals working together, in sync, executing a concept or a play is pure poetry in motion.

But like anything else, it doesn't happen overnight, and it doesn't happen if the point guard is unable to dribble in order to initiate the offense, or if the wings lack confidence to attack a spot on the floor with the dribble. Great execution takes tons of practice. Individuals must commit to working on ball handling and the group must spend time together running through the plays until it becomes second nature.

The real-life application of this takes place in the home, the workplace, in school, in church, with friend groups, etc. The art of passing the basketball signifies our connection with others. The goal is still the same: the hoop (the commitment to Christ). But most of our lives revolve around those we share this life with. Our passes, our connection with others, should set them up to be successful. They should be leading and pointing to the hoop, to Jesus Christ.

Putting aside the pass itself, the use of the dribble is still paramount in creating a multitude of better passes. Again, the dribble is our daily devotion to God in reading and prayer. In order to be effective in our connection with others it is essential to stay fixed on our Creator. Prayer, communication with God, is a continuous act. It should be like breathing, something that takes place in every moment of our day. First Thessalonians 5:17 states, "pray without ceasing."

I have only come close to adhering to this directive, in a literal sense, once in my life. I explained earlier about Beast Barracks at West Point. That summer of basic training for me was a tremendous shock to the system. Most days I recited the simplest of prayers over and over, "God help me." On a given day it would be a conservative estimate to admit that I prayed that prayer three hundred times. It was all I could put together, but it was presented with all my heart. In that situation, I was certainly staying grounded in God, but I'm not sure how I impacted the lives of those around me. I was merely trying to survive.

Ephesians 6:18 expands on this directive: "praying always with all prayer and supplication in the Spirit, being watchful to this end with all perseverance and supplication for all the saints." When we accept Jesus Christ as our Lord and Savior we enter into a relationship that includes the Holy Spirit. The Spirit is the third part of the Trinity with God the Father and Jesus the Son. The Holy Spirit dwells inside the believer and functions on this earth, connecting us with God the Father in heaven. Our prayers, in the Spirit and led by the Spirit, open the dialogue with our Creator. I am no theologian, so I will stop there. My point is we are not merely physical beings, but spiritual ones as well. When we commit to Christ, the Holy Spirit continuously unites us with God. We communicate with God on many levels, including the Spirit leading us in that communion. That connection with our Creator is imperative if we hope to positively affect the lives of those around us.

Over one three year period God moved me into a new role within our family dynamic. I continued to coach, but my day job changed dramatically: I became a stay-at-home dad. My wife and I switched roles, with her returning to the classroom as a full-time teacher. And, in the age of Covid, I also became the technology coordinator for our children's virtual learning needs. I cooked and cleaned and washed dishes. I prepared breakfast, lunch, and snacks. I took them out for our version of physical education and managed the energy of three elementary-age kids. It was a pretty good gig!

Since then, I have found myself in a position of incredible influence over my children almost all of the time. There are many days where our home runs beautifully; poetry in motion. But, there are equally as many where it does not. There are times when I handle a situation pretty well, and there are times when I mess it up. The common denominator in all that goes on during a day is me. This is where my connection to God through reading and prayer really comes into play. If I disconnect and get sloppy with my time with God, our home atmosphere gets a bit sloppy. If I stay plugged into my Creator, the environment stays pretty solid. It's a point of emphasis that demands regular attention—not just day by day, but sometimes minute by minute.

The family unit is much like a basketball team on the court. In my case, the five of us are making passes all the time—some good, some bad—and it has a lot to do with how plugged in each of us is with God. My wife and I set aside our time each day, and we set aside time to do the same with our three kids. Our day includes a Bible story and prayers together. Our oldest is even encouraged to take a little time to start building this habit on his own. In addition, as every parent knows, each of our children has a different personality, with different needs. Our oldest, Xander, is a quality-time kid. He needs some one-on-one time with a parent to fill his tank. Our middle child, Ollie, is pretty big on physical contact. Chilling together on the couch, a wrestling session, or a hug do the trick most of the time. And our youngest, Isla Grace, is still one we are figuring out. She's very affectionate and loves a good cuddle, so we enjoy making that happen. These examples are put in simplest form but highlight the point that every individual has specific needs that need to be met in order for them to operate at an optimum level.

As parents, when we facilitate our children's connection with God and intentionally set aside time to meet their individual needs the home runs more smoothly. When we flunk, the road gets bumpy. And all of this is predicated on that daily discipline of reading and prayer. The connection with God gives us insight into the needs of our children, as well as the needs of others. It allows us to know what kind of pass is needed to help set them up to be successful. We are able to create better passes when grounded in a daily commitment to Christ. But, just like basketball, there are some gorgeous moments and some truly ugly ones. The key is to just keep plugging away.

PART THREE

PASSING

CHAPTER 8

THE BOUNCE PASS

Passing the basketball has always been my favorite aspect of the offensive game. I love how it connects teammates while also moving the defense. The extra pass, hitting the open man, is a thing of beauty. It signifies unselfishness at such a high level. And I love how the pass is a perfect representation of the interactions between human beings. A lot can be learned about life just by watching a squad that is gifted at passing. Maybe even better, tons can be learned while watching a team that doesn't share the ball well.

During the summer of 2020 I had the opportunity to watch more NBA basketball than I had in years. The Orlando Bubble was well put together, and provided a nice escape from Covid life. I quickly fell in love with one team, and one player in particular. Nicola Jokic and the Denver Nuggets were fun to watch. I so appreciate the skill level Jokic possesses. What he lacks in athleticism he more than makes up for in fundamental proficiency. He has a good shot, he can handle the ball, and he is an excellent passer. I have no doubt his teammates love playing with him. He consistently makes the next right play. Our household became such fans that we purchased Ollie a Nuggets hat and Jokic shirt for his birthday. I threw in one for myself as well.

Passing the ball symbolizes our communication and interaction with others. It can set people up for success or put them in a really bad spot. It can lead to a made bucket or result in a turnover. Our words and actions are the same way. They can lift others up, encouraging them and bringing joy into their life, or they can tear down, humiliate, and produce despair. The ability to encourage or discourage lies within our control. There are countless opportunities every day to make good passes, and it's important to know what kind of pass to use when the time comes.

The bounce pass requires a combination of precision and finesse in the midst of heavy defensive traffic. The entire point of using the bounce pass is to avoid the active hands of the opposing team. It is an indispensable tool to set up a teammate around the basket. The bounce pass was a crucial part of my game. Anyone that played with me could expect a bounce pass around the rim.

Our starting point guard at Whitworth, Rowan Anderson, is a fantastic young man. He is reliable and dependable on and off the court. He has really stepped up as our team's leader. Rowan is now in his final year in the program. In previous seasons there were moments when he struggled taking care of the basketball.

At one particular practice two seasons ago, I noticed Rowan trying to force too many passes in congested areas. Inevitably, most would get tipped, resulting in turnovers. After practice I pulled him aside and shared my philosophy on passing in the lane. I explained that I used the bounce pass exclusively when passing to a teammate in a scoring position anywhere near the hoop. In my experience I always found it hard for the defense to track and always allowed my teammates to catch the ball unobstructed. Rowan nodded, coachable as always.

Starting the next day, I witnessed Rowan laying out bounce pass after bounce pass in the lane. His turnovers decreased and his assists went up. His passes were caught cleanly and his teammates were in good positions to score. I immediately praised him and continue to praise him every time he completes a great bounce pass.

Not many bounce passes make *SportsCenter*'s nightly Top 10 list, although some could. Not many find their way into highlight reels, although many should. And not many bring a packed arena to its feet, although maybe they ought to. It is the unsung hero of passing, and maybe that is the case because it has so little to do with the person passing and so much more to do with its intention for the recipient.

Philippians 2:3–4 reads, "Let nothing be done through selfish ambition or conceit, but in lowliness of mind let each esteem others better than himself. Let each of you look out not only for his own interests, but also for the interests of others." In basketball, the bounce pass is about timing and setting up a teammate to shine. It is not about pizzazz or providing a "Wow!" factor for the passer. The intention is for the receiver to be successful. These verses in Philippians encapsulate the bounce pass for me.

And in the arena of life, the bounce pass is the timely word to a friend in need, the encouragement one's child requires, the pat on the back, the hug, or maybe just being there for someone else. It is taking the opportunity to lift another person up and truly share Christ's love with them.

The word "edify" means to instruct, to build another up and/or to uplift. It places in my mind the idea of setting someone up for success. First Thessalonians 5:11 states, "Therefore comfort each other and edify one another, just as you also are doing." It is a directive for our daily interactions with others. As Christians we are to take opportunities to lift up and encourage others. Words are powerful, and the right words for the benefit of another can be life changing. They can spur one on to success or encourage them just enough in times that require perseverance. It comes down to truly caring about someone else and being led by the Holy Spirit to express that sentiment.

CHAPTER 9

THE CHEST PASS

Again, passing is the metaphor for our interactions with others. The bounce pass is applicable in heavy-traffic situations involving multiple defenders. The part to now take note of is that of the defenders on the basketball court. The defense symbolizes the adversity we face in life, whether it be from specific individuals, circumstances, or even the thoughts and strongholds in our own minds. In any case, the defenders are pawns of the enemy. As God is our goal and target, and our walk with Him is depicted in the game of basketball, Satan and his forces constitute the defense getting in the way.

Bounce passes work in crowded situations, be it a clogged lane on the court or an overwhelmed friend in everyday life. Other times, we need a quicker, more direct pass to set a teammate up for success. The chest pass symbolizes fast, direct interaction with others. Proverbs 17:17 tells us, "A friend loves at all times, and a brother is born for adversity." I love this verse, as it fits seamlessly in the context of both life and sport. Adversity is always lurking, and it is paramount to have loved ones on your side, ready to go through the fire with you. Even in the mundane moments of life little obstacles arise in our path, and the right action, word, or deed helps to strengthen our resolve.

Friends, parents, and spouses are uniquely positioned to provide the push we often need. Hebrews 10:24 clarifies this positioning: "And let us consider one another in order to stir up love and good works." We do not walk alone in this life, and Christians are instructed to operate in community. We are given the task to "stir up" others to do the right thing. We are to hold one another accountable, chastening each other when we veer off course, and celebrating when we stay on it. Quick, decisive communication can make the difference in someone's day. And it is so important to be surrounded by those that provide accountability in this life.

Titus 3:14 instructs: "And let our people also learn to maintain good works, to meet urgent needs, that they may not be unfruitful." We are to be vessels that meet the needs of others. Sometimes it's just being there in the face of dire circumstances (maybe a bounce pass moment), or it may be pointed instruction to help tackle a situation (chest pass). In either case, we are to be lights in the darkness and set others up for success.

At the end of my senior year in high school I was selected to participate in two state-wide all-star basketball games. The two experiences could not have been more different. The first game was the Scott Brown Memorial Classic, which pitted all-state players from

AAA against all-state players from AA and A classifications. I found myself having to play an undefined role alongside a very ball-dominant guard. As the game wore on it became evident that the four of us on the court with this player were just there in case he decided to throw us the ball. What stood out the most was I often found myself receiving a pass from him in a position that set me up to fail. He would drive in the lane against four defenders, and at the last minute toss it to me in a crowd where I was completely boxed in. I was left helpless and clueless as to what I was supposed to accomplish. It was a very frustrating experience.

In the second fixture, the North-South All-Star Game, I was a member of all-state players from the northern half of the state. A friend of mine, Sean Skubis, was also named to the roster. We attended different high schools at different classifications, so never played one another during our high school careers. But we were from the same town and grew up together. The last time we were teammates was at Miller Junior High School, where we won the county championship. We hadn't seen each other in years, but now found ourselves riding down together for this event.

It was so much fun to play with Sean. He took the primary ball handling responsibilities for our team, but in a totally different way than my previous experience. Sean was a smart, extremely unselfish player. He knew his role was to facilitate so others could score. I would run the court and, sure enough, the ball would be in my hands quickly, allowing me room to operate and attack my defender. Sean got me the ball early and often, not holding onto it to attempt something spectacular. Instead, he put me in a position to be successful. As a direct result, I was awarded MVP for our team, and Sean had a ton to do with that.

These polar-opposite experiences highlight my point about the chest pass. In the first example, the ball-dominant player was only interested in making highlight plays. When he did pass the ball, I was in no position to be successful. I would compare this to someone that offers advice after the fact, or to someone who leaves a person hanging when in need. They fail to see the need of another or how to communicate in a way to encourage, edify, or strengthen that person, and thus fail to meet the Titus imperative of maintaining good works or meeting the needs of others.

Sean, in the second example, provided clear and quick chest passes in space, allowing me to attack the basket with confidence. He was unselfish, understanding the needs of others and how best to set them up. He was not in it for glory, but in it as a teammate, trying to do what was best for all. To me this exemplifies someone bringing a necessary word before it's too late and truly caring about another's well-being. This is what we are called to do as Christians. We are called to speak clearly and directly in the interest of others. We are to be friends that are present through the adversity. We are to stir up love and good works in ourselves and others.

PART FOUR

RECEIVING THE PASS

CHAPTER 10

TRIPLE THREAT

Xander, Ollie, and I continue to spend significant time in the spring and summer working on basketball. I do a ton of rebounding and passing so the two of them can get shots up and improve their skills. The last foundational component to their individual success is receiving the pass in the proper manner. We use the terms "hop turn" and "pivot turn" to signify two ways to catch the ball. Both boys being right-handed, they will catch the ball coming one direction with a left foot down as they pivot while turning to face the basket. From the other direction, each will hop and turn in the air while receiving the pass, landing with both feet down at the same time and facing the basket. I emphasize balance and control as they each catch the ball. This puts them in "triple-threat" position as they can then shoot, pass, or dribble. The balanced positioning of triple-threat is a posture of strength, emphasizing 1 Corinthians 16:13: "Watch, stand fast in the faith, be brave, be strong."

It is so important to be on balance in the game of basketball, just as it is in our walk with the Lord. When we stand strong, with our heads up, eyeing the situation, we are ready to face whatever adversity comes our way. In Ephesians, we are instructed to put on the armor of God, which again is a mandate of preparedness. Ephesians 6:10 directs, "Finally, my brethren, be strong in the Lord and in the power of His might." Paul begins with this directive before breaking down the importance of each individual piece of spiritual armor. These words paint a picture of balance and strength, rooted in our relationship with God. And, in the metaphor of a triple threat, I like to picture the pivot foot as that root.

I instruct my sons that the left foot (while on the perimeter) is the pivot foot for each of them. Again, that is based on them both being right-handed. The left foot is the root, connected to the court. It is the base of operations from which to make the appropriate offensive read. From this basis, Xander and Ollie go through a series of jab movements aimed at shifting the primary defender in order to create space. Each will jab right to drive left, jab left to drive right, and then jab to create space for a shot. In Scripture, we are instructed to "test" all things in order to know what is of God. First Thessalonians 5:21 orders, "Test all things; hold fast to what is good." And 1 John 4:1 urges, "Beloved, do not believe every spirit, but test the spirits, whether they are of God; because many false prophets have gone out into the world." The jab is the testing. The primary defender is our roadblock in life. It could be a situation we are facing, a person that has become an obstacle in our lives, an addiction, or some other attack against us or a loved one. What we do know is that God is the bucket and something is in the way.

In basketball, the jab functions to displace the defender and make a clear path for our success. We can "test" the defender in order to find out what our appropriate path should be. In life, the jab includes time in prayer, in reading God's Word, in discussions with spiritual leaders, and in listening and waiting on the Lord. We must "test" what's in front of us, relying on God to make our path clear.

The second way to test the defender is to use the shot fake. While still maintaining a posture of strength in triple-threat position, lifting the ball in the initial movements of the shooting motion may cause the defender to react and attempt to block the shot. If so, the offensive player has successfully compromised the defender by taking the opponent out of a defensive stance. At this point, options for driving the basketball become apparent because the defender is no longer prepared and in the way. Similar to the jab step, the defender has been moved in order to create a clear path through which to drive the basketball.

And the last way to test the defender is with the use of a pass fake. Making timely movements, faking a pass to the left, right, or across the court can not only shift the primary defender on the basketball, but also the rest of the defenders guarding the basket. Again, this test is intended to weaken the defender(s) and create passing or driving lanes. A great pass fake can move all five defenders and open up incredible scoring opportunities.

The jab step, the shot fake, and the pass fake are all ways to test the defense and make clear which path to take. To properly use each of these three skills, one must start from a position of strength. Triple-threat is that position of strength in basketball. It provides balance, composure, and confidence in the midst of chaos. In this life, our relationship with the Lord provides that same balance, composure, and confidence we need. The pivot foot is rooted in God, supplying the source of strength to weather the surroundings. James 1:5 reads, "If any of you lacks wisdom, let him ask of God, who gives to all liberally and without reproach, and it will be given to him." We have so many assurances that God is with us and for us and ready to supply in all circumstances. It is our responsibility to stay in that humble posture, seeking Him and asking of Him on a daily basis. He will provide.

It is recorded in Exodus 15:2:

> "The Lord is my strength and song,
> And He has become my salvation;
> He is my God, and I will praise Him;
> My father's God, and I will exalt Him."

This is a portion of a song sung by Moses and the Israelites. These words ring as true today as they did thousands of years ago. It is my song to the Lord, for He is my strength and He is my father's God as well.

At the heart of these pages is the desire for my children to walk always in the strength of the Lord, exemplifying and passing on this relationship with the Lord to their children. My boys love basketball (my daughter, we shall see) and I pray these metaphors speak to their hearts and provide a depth and understanding that goes well beyond the game itself.

Thank You

To the Women in My Life

To Mom:
Thank you for always being my biggest fan. You've prayed for me since before my birth, and I know every single day that you are still doing the same. You've cheered me on as I played the game throughout my youth, often having to leave the gym because you became so nervous watching. You have always been ready to listen and support me through my struggles, and you continue to do so. While these stories have many references to Dad, I know you were no less valuable in my growth and development. There is nothing more powerful than a prayer warrior behind the scenes. Thank you.

To Heather:
When I picture my playing days, I picture you with your big glasses on, hanging at the end of the bench, helping with water. You always had a smile, and the pride in your face gave me so much confidence. I know you got tired of many visits in grocery stores, doctor's offices, etc. ending in conversations about my basketball career. Thank you for enduring that. I'm so grateful you have such a loving husband and so excited

to maybe one day have a role to play in pouring into Jett's life through the game of basketball.

To Katy:

I would not be where I am today without your love and support. We've been through some fires that I would not trade for anything. The struggles have always brought us closer to God and closer to one another. You've blessed me with three amazing children and a life that gives me excitement each and every day. Thank you for being such a wonderful wife and mother. Thank you for being my best friend.

To Isla Grace:

I've saved you for last because your footprint in these pages is not evident. I do not know yet if the game of basketball is for you. What I do know is that you have been the most amazing "Whitworth Girl." Your preschool years were spent in the Fieldhouse, impacting every Whitworth practice in some way. You had Coach Logie wrapped around your finger on day one, you were instrumental in melting the hearts of recruits and their parents, and Coach Jablonski was quite lost without you for some time when you started kindergarten. You hold a special place in the hearts of Coach Hurst and Coach Love, as well as those of numerous players. The joy that is inherent in you is nothing short of amazing. You are an encourager and a ray of light. You and I together, going to and from college basketball practices, is a most precious memory. I cannot imagine it without you. I will pour into you through the game of basketball as I do with your brothers should that be the path you choose. If you choose another path, I will be a part of it, making memories with you and supporting you and pouring into your life with all my heart. You are such a blessing to me. Thank you. I love you.

About the Author

Elijah Gurash has been a collegiate basketball coach since 2018, after having spent fifteen years in the high school ranks. He holds a Bachelor of Arts degree from Northwest Christian University (now Bushnell University) and a Master of Science degree from The University of Edinburgh. Elijah and his wife, Katy, have three children: Xander, Oliver and Isla Grace.

www.ingramcontent.com/pod-product-compliance
Lightning Source LLC
LaVergne TN
LVHW010602070526
838199LV00063BA/5047